THERE'S SOMETHING IN THE WATER!

Marine Biology for Kids Children's Biology Books

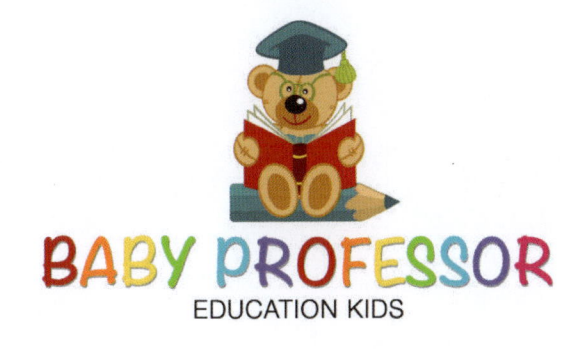

BABY PROFESSOR
EDUCATION KIDS

Speedy Publishing LLC

40 E. Main St. #1156

Newark, DE 19711

www.speedypublishing.com

Copyright 2017

All Rights reserved. No part of this book may be reproduced or used in any way or form or by any means whether electronic or mechanical, this means that you cannot record or photocopy any material ideas or tips that are provided in this book

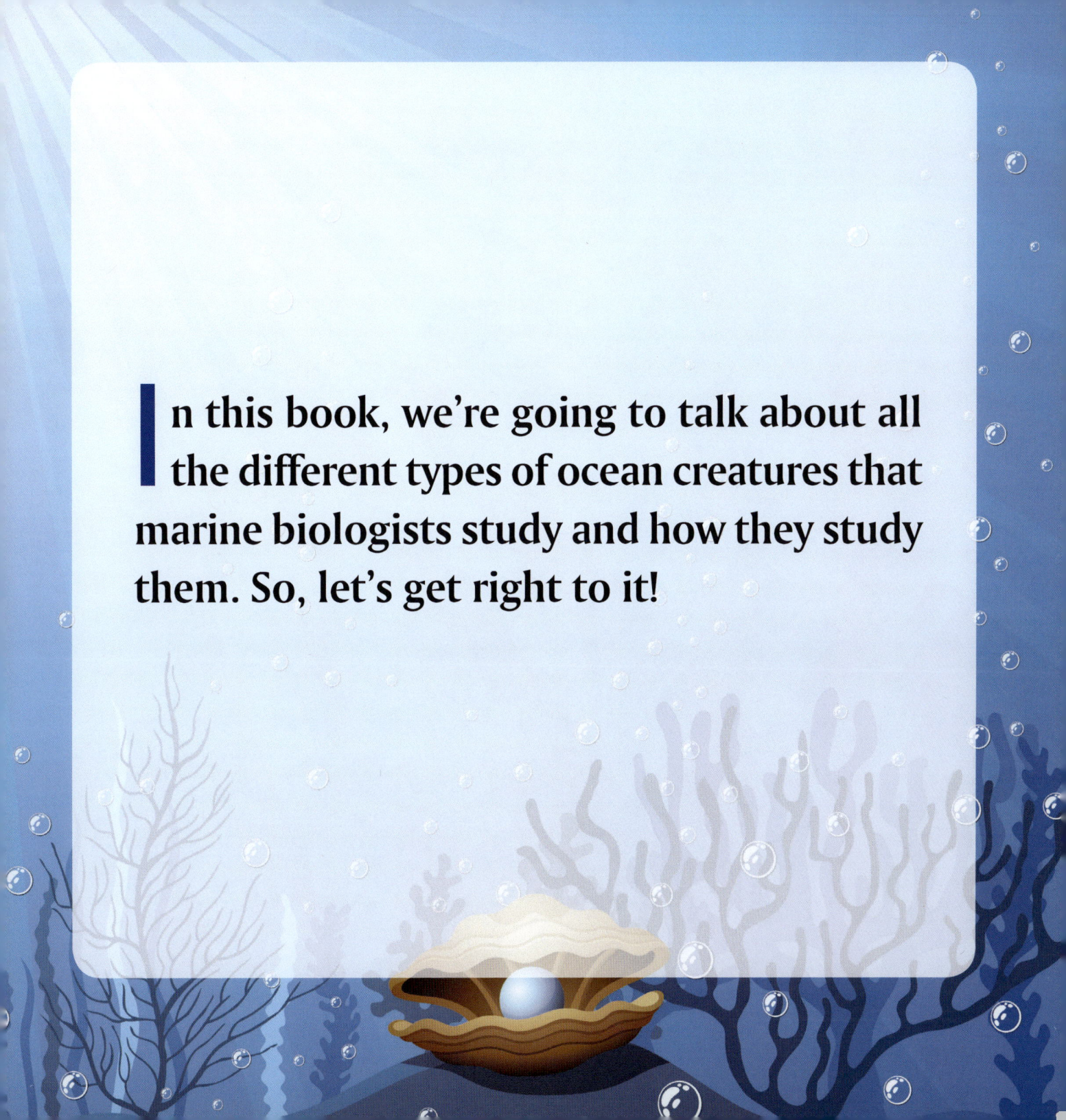

In this book, we're going to talk about all the different types of ocean creatures that marine biologists study and how they study them. So, let's get right to it!

OCEAN LIFE

Life began in the ocean over 3.1 billion years ago. Organisms didn't appear on land until 400 million years ago, so it's clear that all life on Earth evolved from marine life. Because of their surface area as well as their depth, the oceans make up 99% of the living space on planet Earth. In fact, it's estimated that up to 80% of all life on Earth lives in the oceans.

The oceans are teeming with so much life that it's hard to imagine it. A fish that swallows a mouthful of salt water isn't just swallowing water. It's swallowing bacteria in the millions, phytoplankton in the hundred of thousands, and zooplankton in the tens of thousands.

Many organisms that live in the oceans are surrounded by water all of their lives. They don't even know that there is a sky or land on Earth.

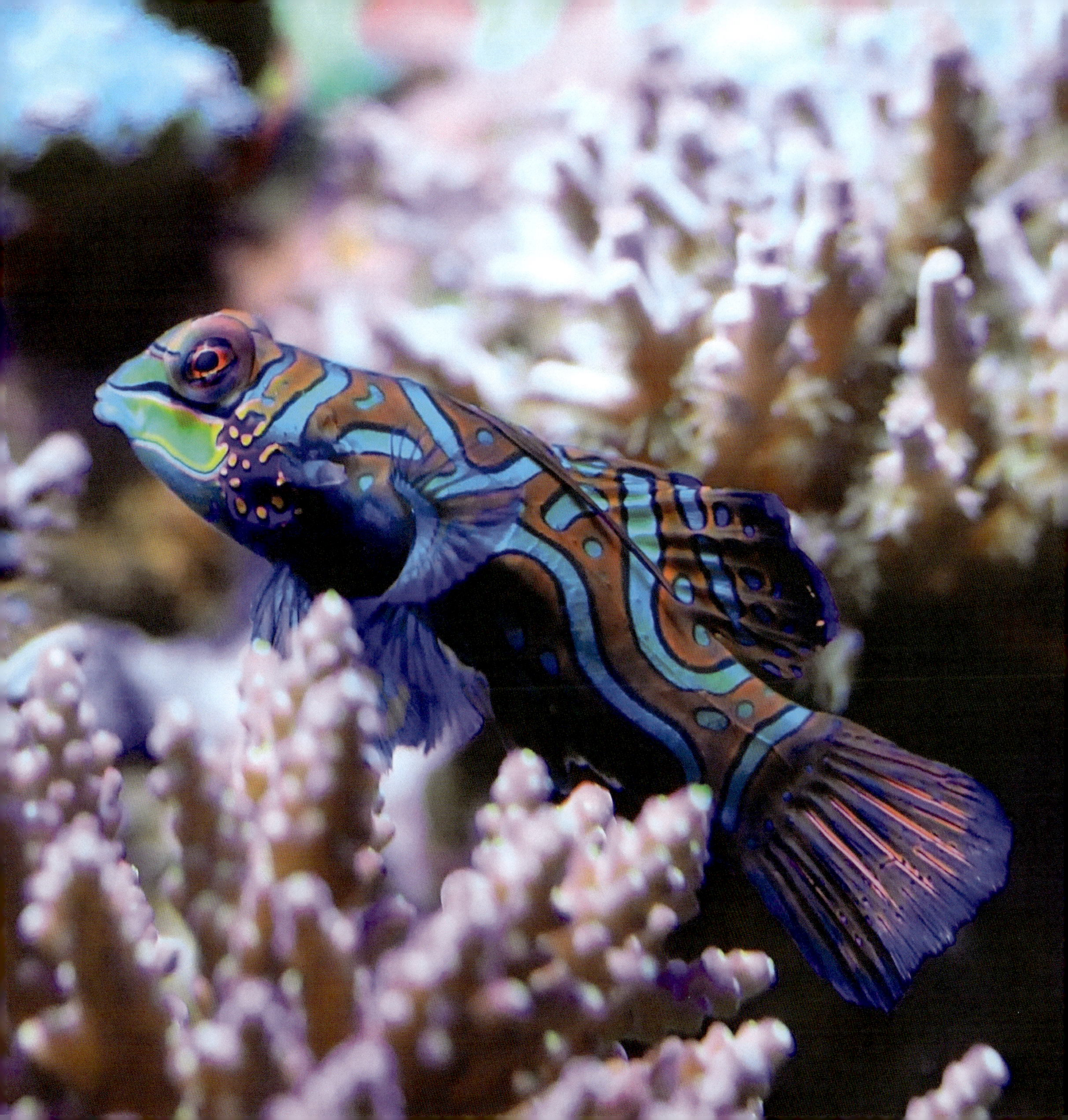

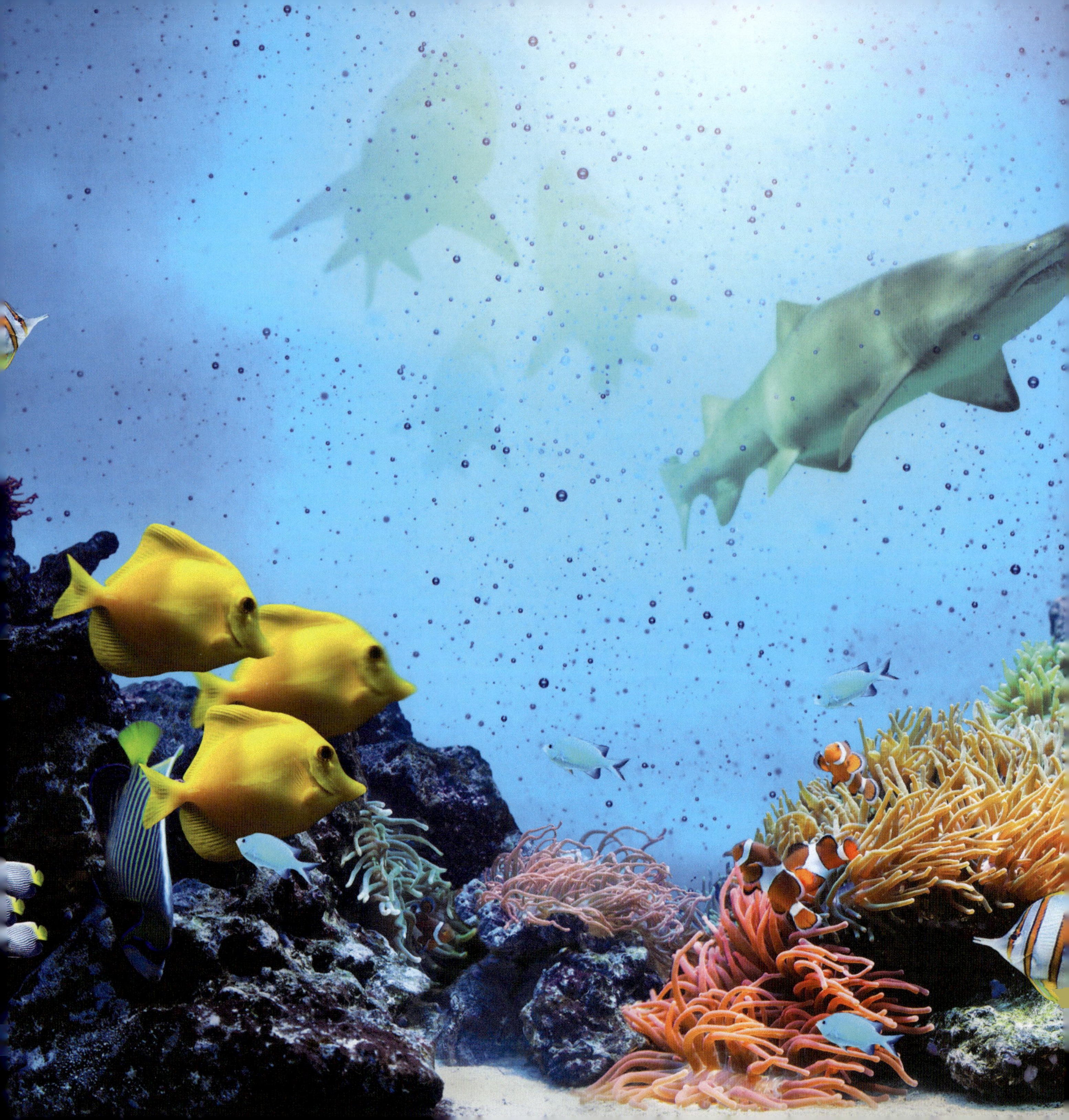

WHAT IS MARINE BIOLOGY?

Marine biology is the study of ocean life. Marine biologists study all the different types of plants and animals that thrive in saltwater.

Every creature from the tiniest microbe to the enormous blue whale, which is the largest animal in the world, is important to the marine biologist.

COURSE OF STUDY FOR MARINE BIOLOGY

In order to become a marine biologist, you'll need to study lots of different subjects. Here are some of the subjects you will need to master:

- **Zoology,** the study of animals
- **Chemistry,** the study of chemical reactions
- **Geology,** the study of rock formations
- **Ecology,** the study of ecosystems
- **Botany,** the study of plants
- **Oceanography,** the study of oceans

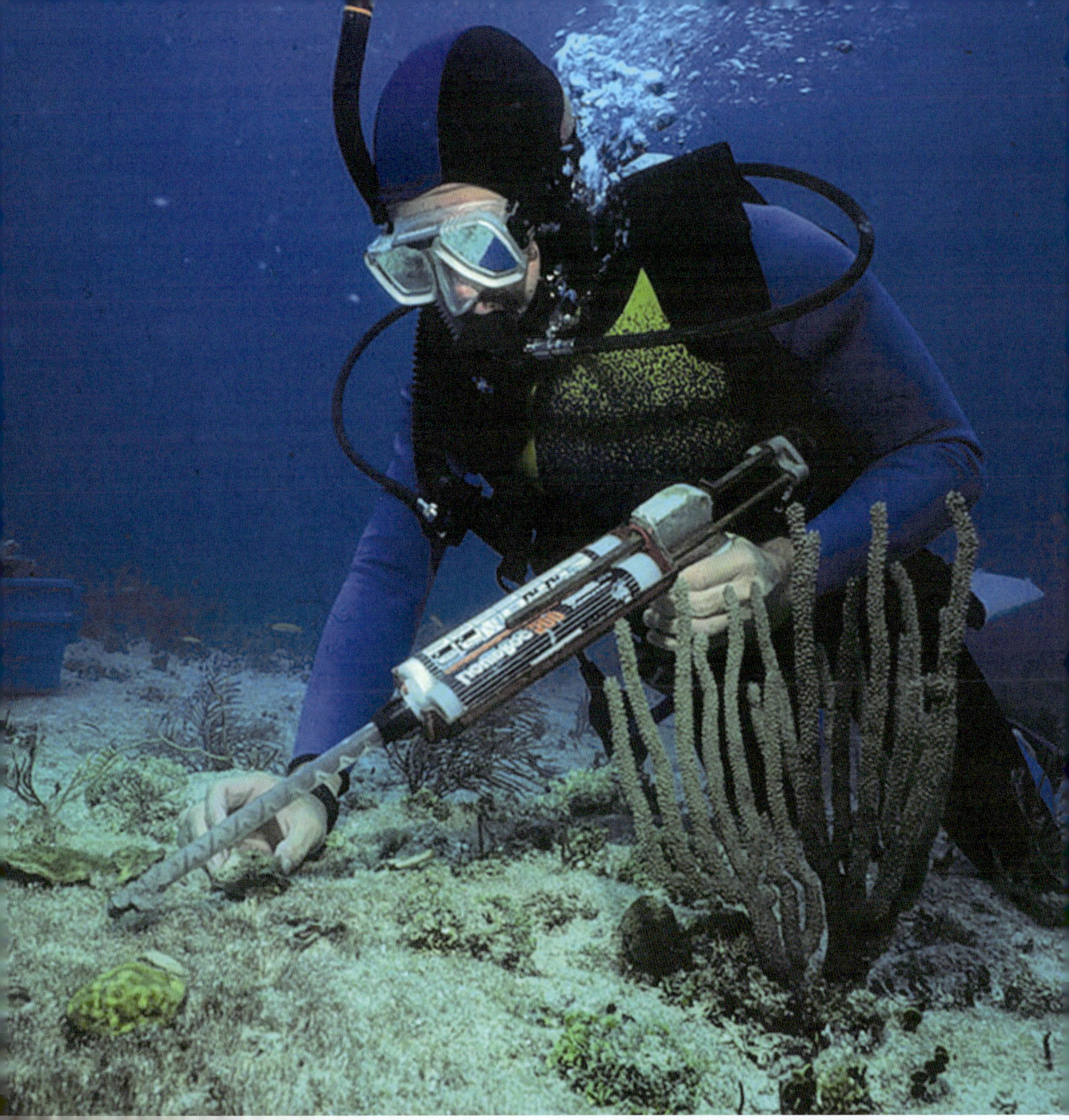

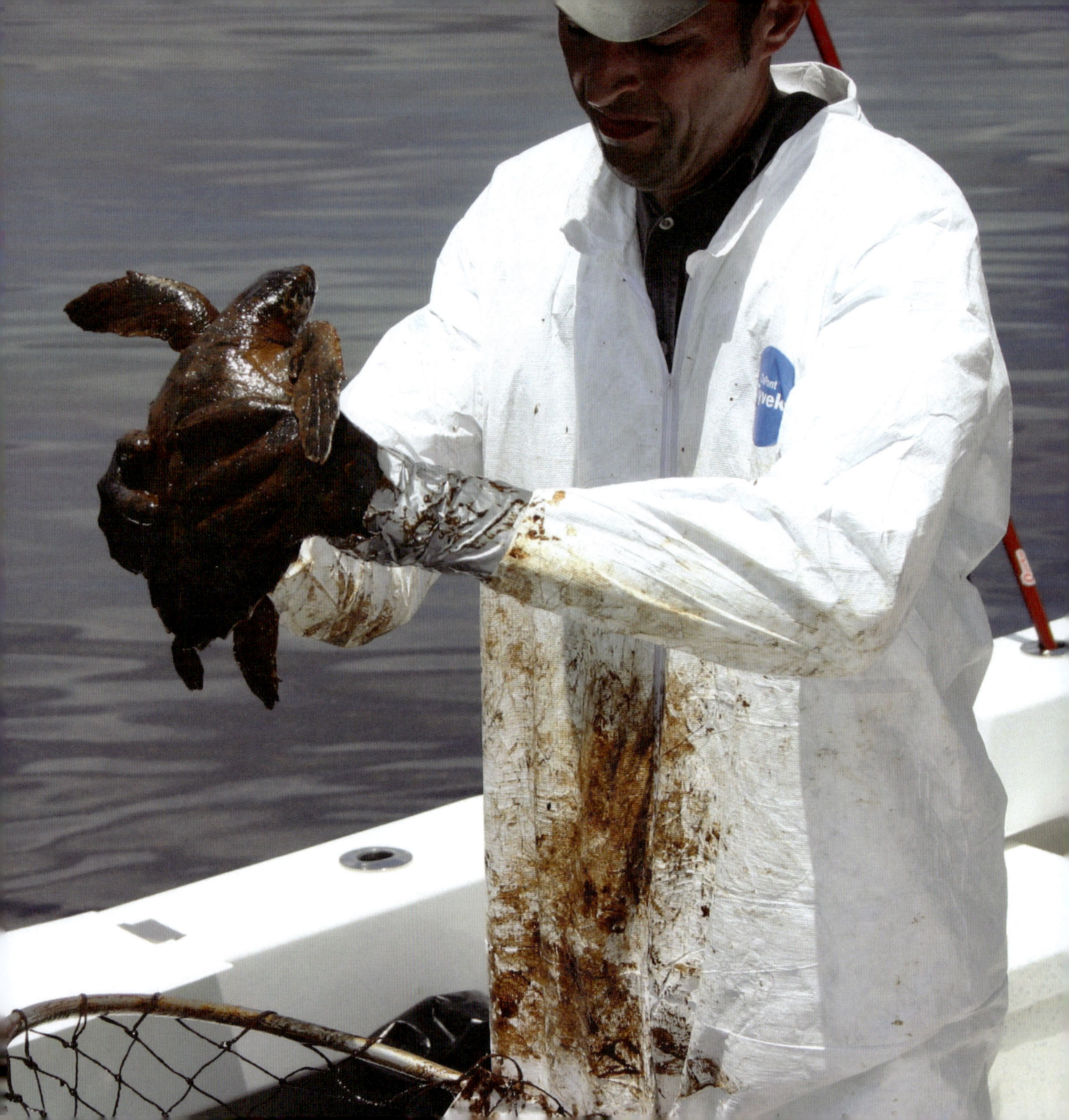

HOW ARE MARINE LIFE FORMS STUDIED?

A marine biologist is a specific type of scientist. Just like all scientists, marine biologists depend on a process called the scientific method. All scientists want the same thing.

They want to find out the truth. In order to determine whether something is true or not true, marine biologists set up experiments to test their theories.

For example, let's say you were studying a certain type of octopus. When you're underwater observing the octopus, you notice that it carries shiny objects back to its den. You also notice that this octopus is a male and that the female octopus seems to select him over other males.

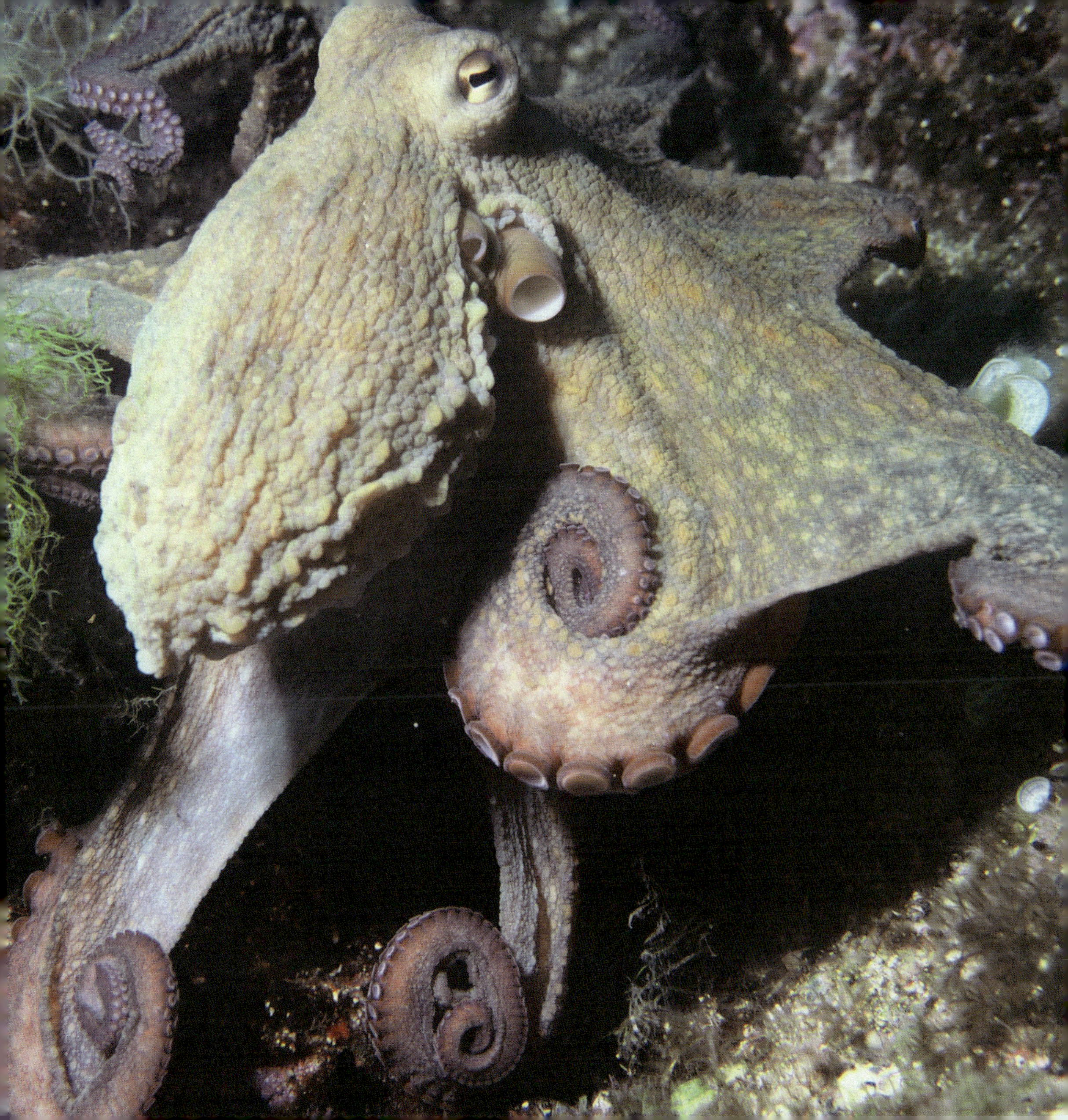

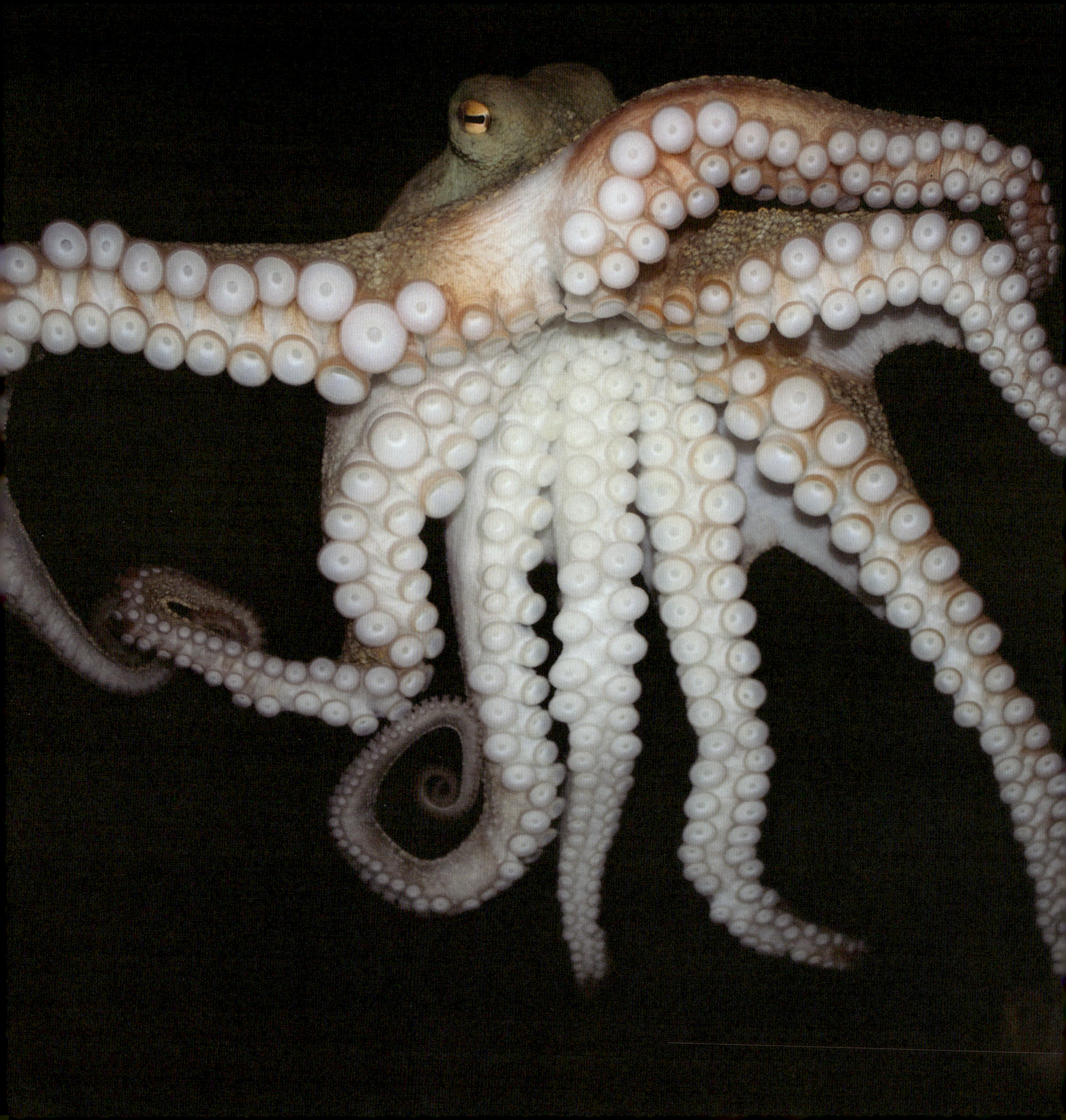

He has more colorful shiny objects in his collection that the other octopuses so she chooses him to be her mate. Before you could conclude that the male octopus is gathering these colorful objects to attract a mate, you would need to set up an experiment.

Here are the steps in the scientific method you would use.

- **Characterization,** you notice by observation what the octopus is doing
- **Hypothesis,** you think there's a reason for his behavior
- **Prediction,** you predict that there's a relationship between the number and quality of shiny objects in his den and his ability to attract mates
- **Experiment,** you'll need to set up an experiment that will test your theory to see if it's correct

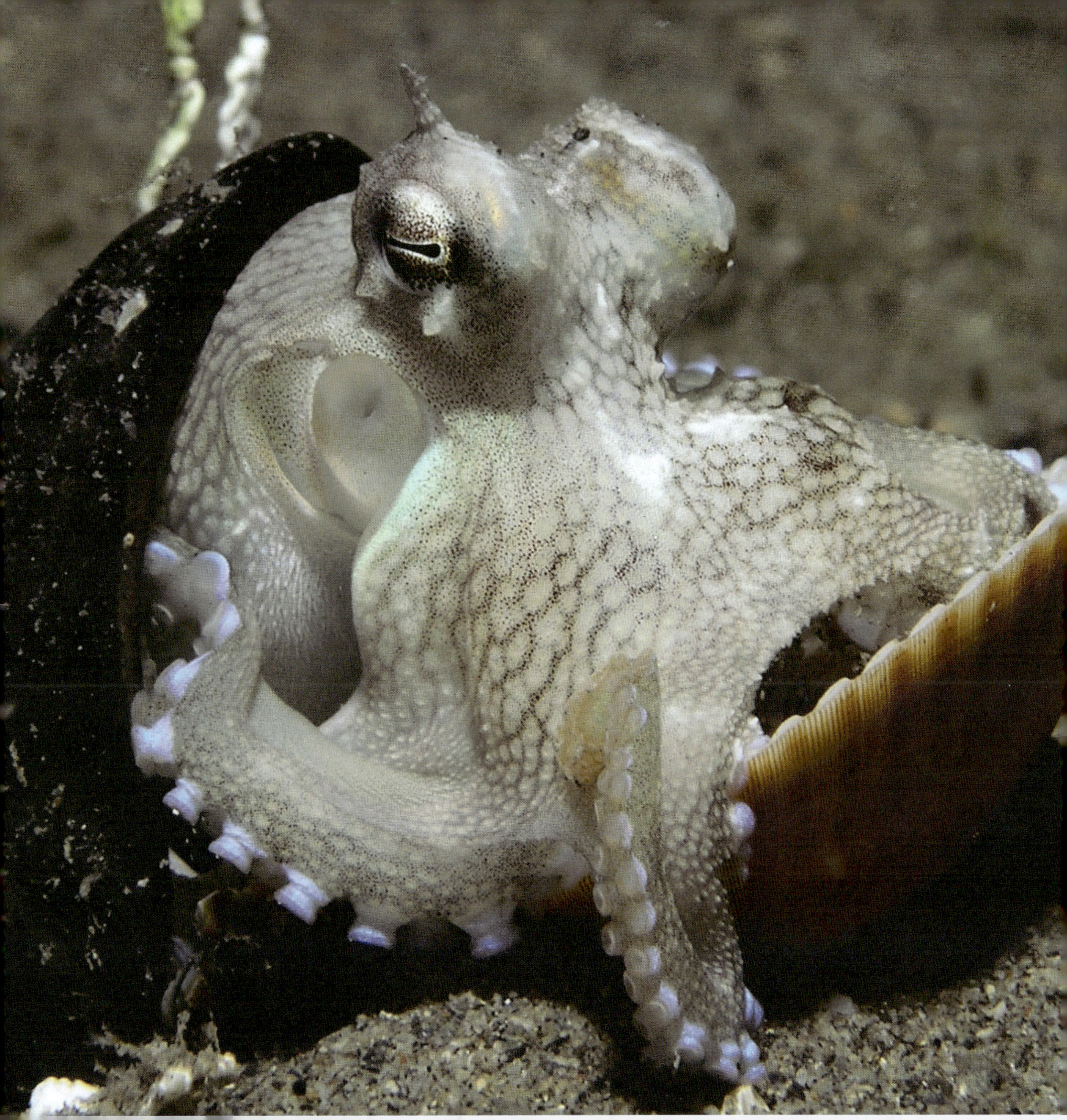

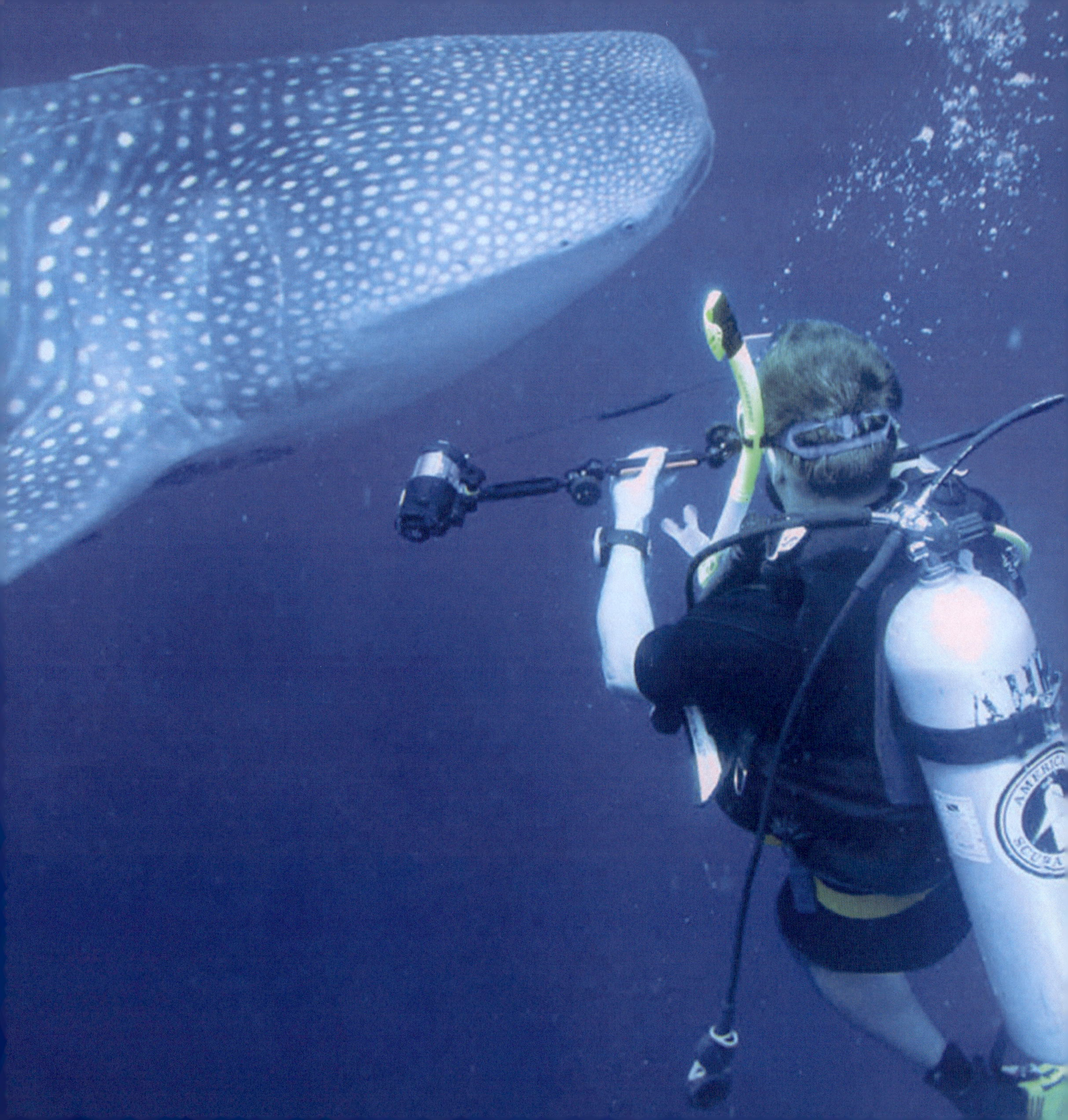

Once you get some results, other marine biologists will test your findings as well. There's always a chance that the experiment got results that weren't correct so others will need to be able to repeat your experiment or one like it to see if they get the same results.

MARINE BIOLOGY SPECIALTY AREAS

Most marine biologists specialize in a specific area of microbiology. The oceans are so vast and there's so much to know that no one individual can know all the subcategories of marine biology.

Here are some of the major fields for research:

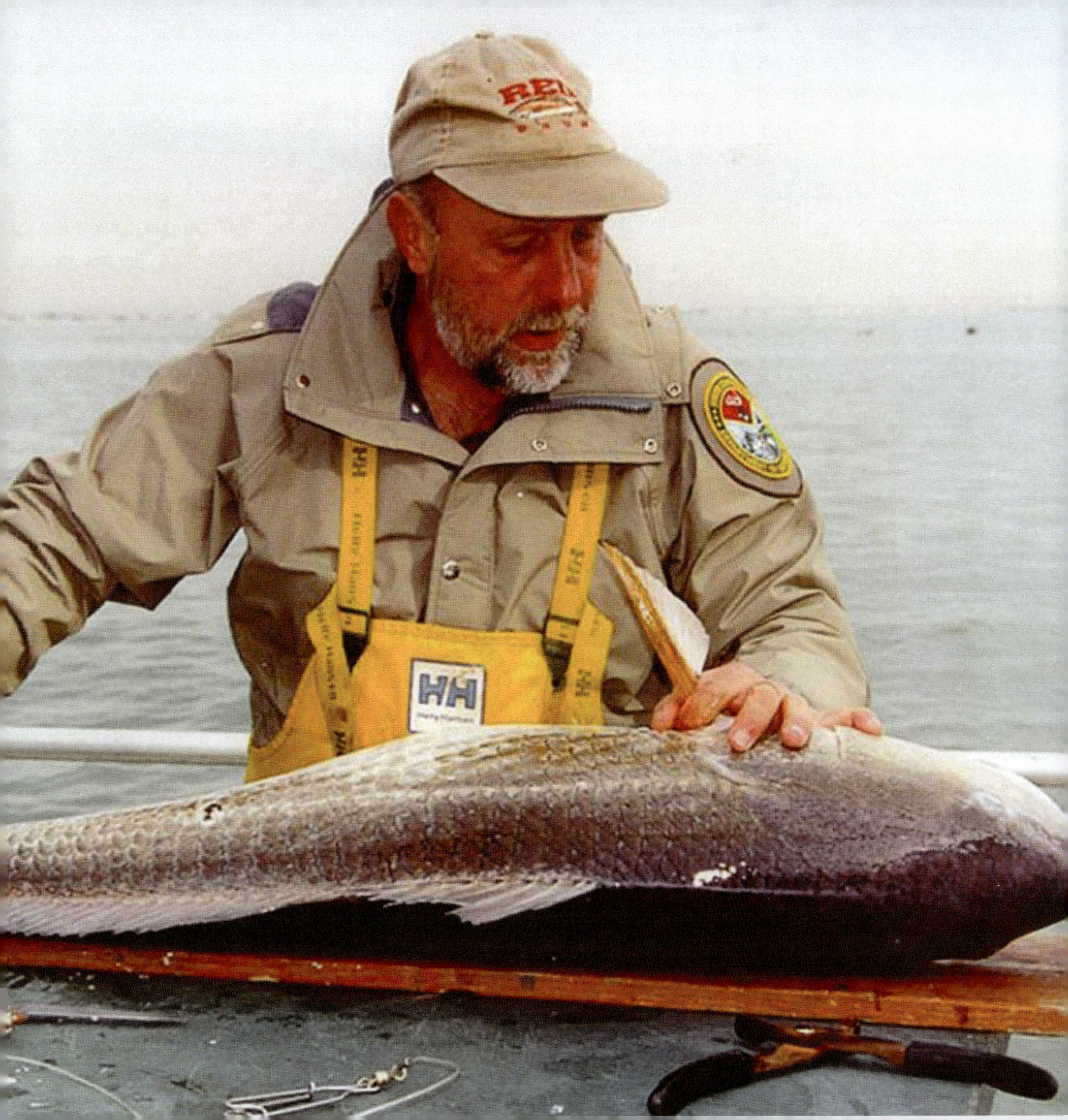
HH

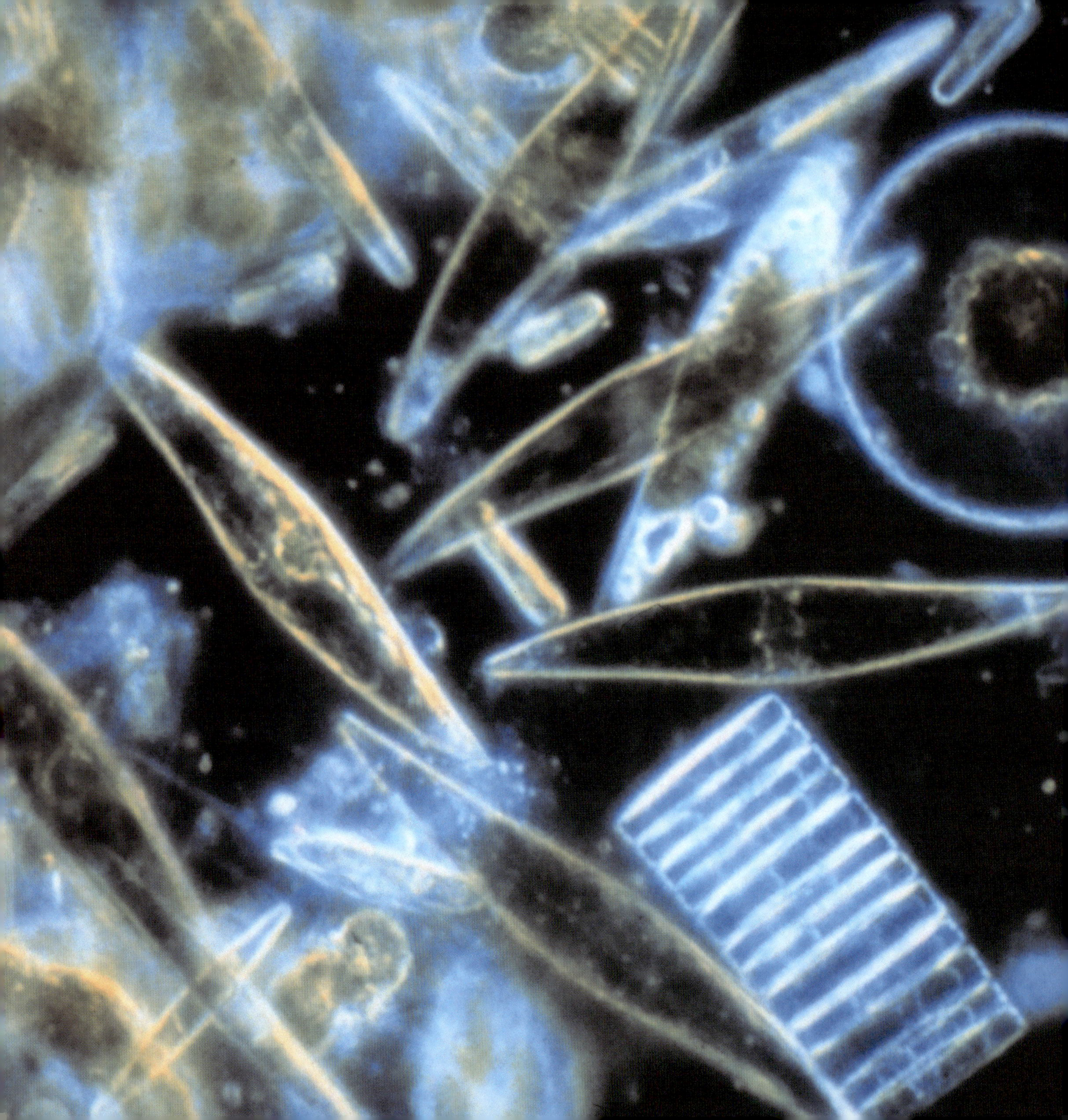

MICROBIOLOGY

Microorganisms, such as bacteria, algae, and protozoa, are vital to marine ecosystems. They are the beginning of the food chain that impacts all ocean animals.

Microorganisms make up 98% of the biomass of the ocean, which means that they are 98% of the total weight of all ocean organisms.

FISHERIES AND AQUACULTURE

This area of study is about creating sustainable sources of food through commercial fisheries as well as high-tech seafood farms. Fish and other seafood are important food sources.

ENVIRONMENTAL MARINE BIOLOGY

The marine biologists in this field are dedicated to keeping our oceans healthy and free of toxins.

Aquaculture pen

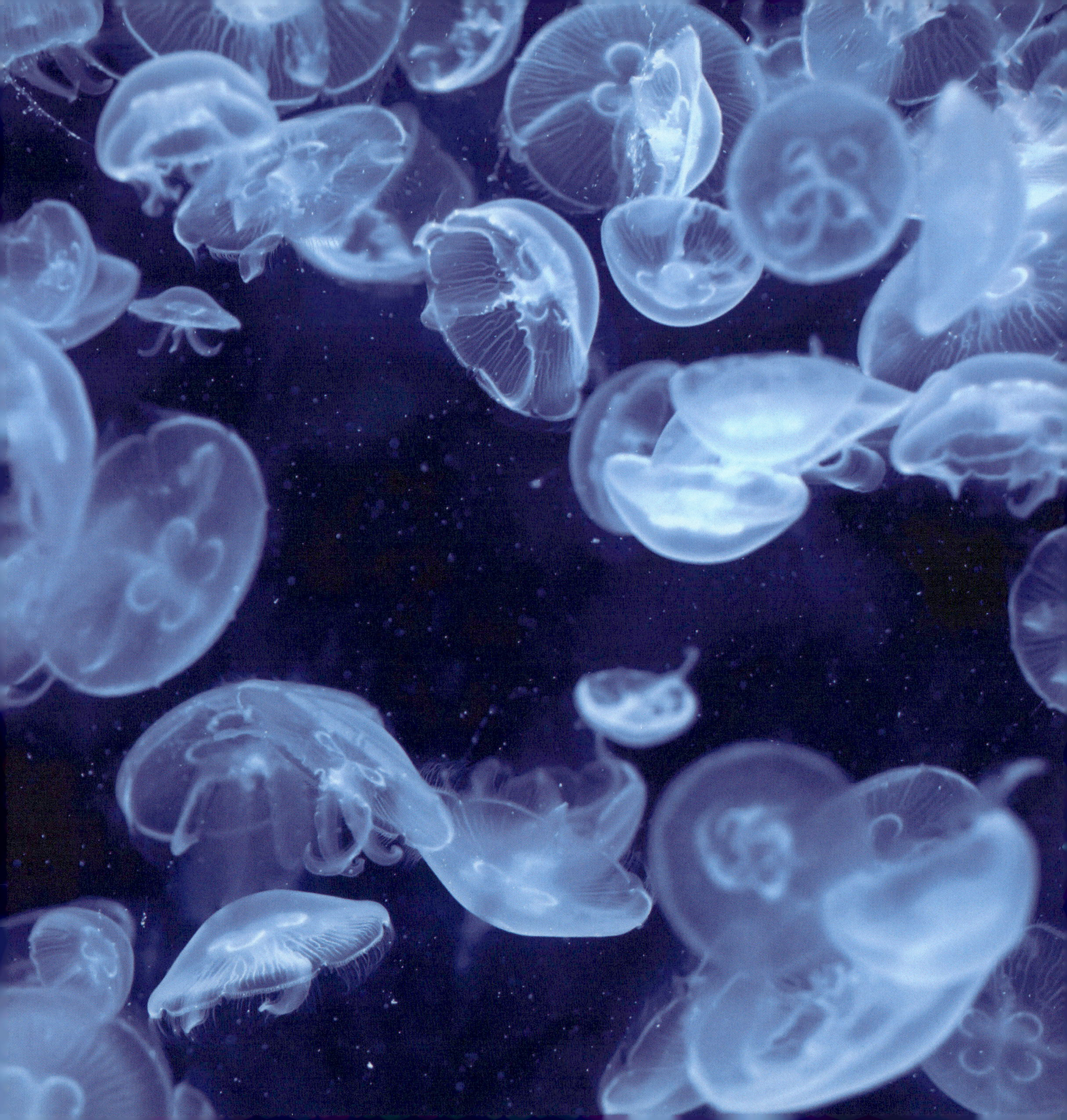

DEEP-SEA ECOLOGY

In this area of study, marine biologists research the deepest part of the ocean. Ocean creatures that live at these depths have adapted to the high pressures and cold temperatures of this environment.

Some of these creatures make their own light through a process called bioluminescence. Other areas of interest to these marine biologists are hydrothermal vents and the communities of life that congregate around them.

ICHTHYOLOGY

Ichthyology is the study of all types of fishes. There are over 25,000 fish species in categories such as bony fish, fish with cartilage skeletons, and jawless fishes. They study everything from classification of fish to their evolution and behavior.

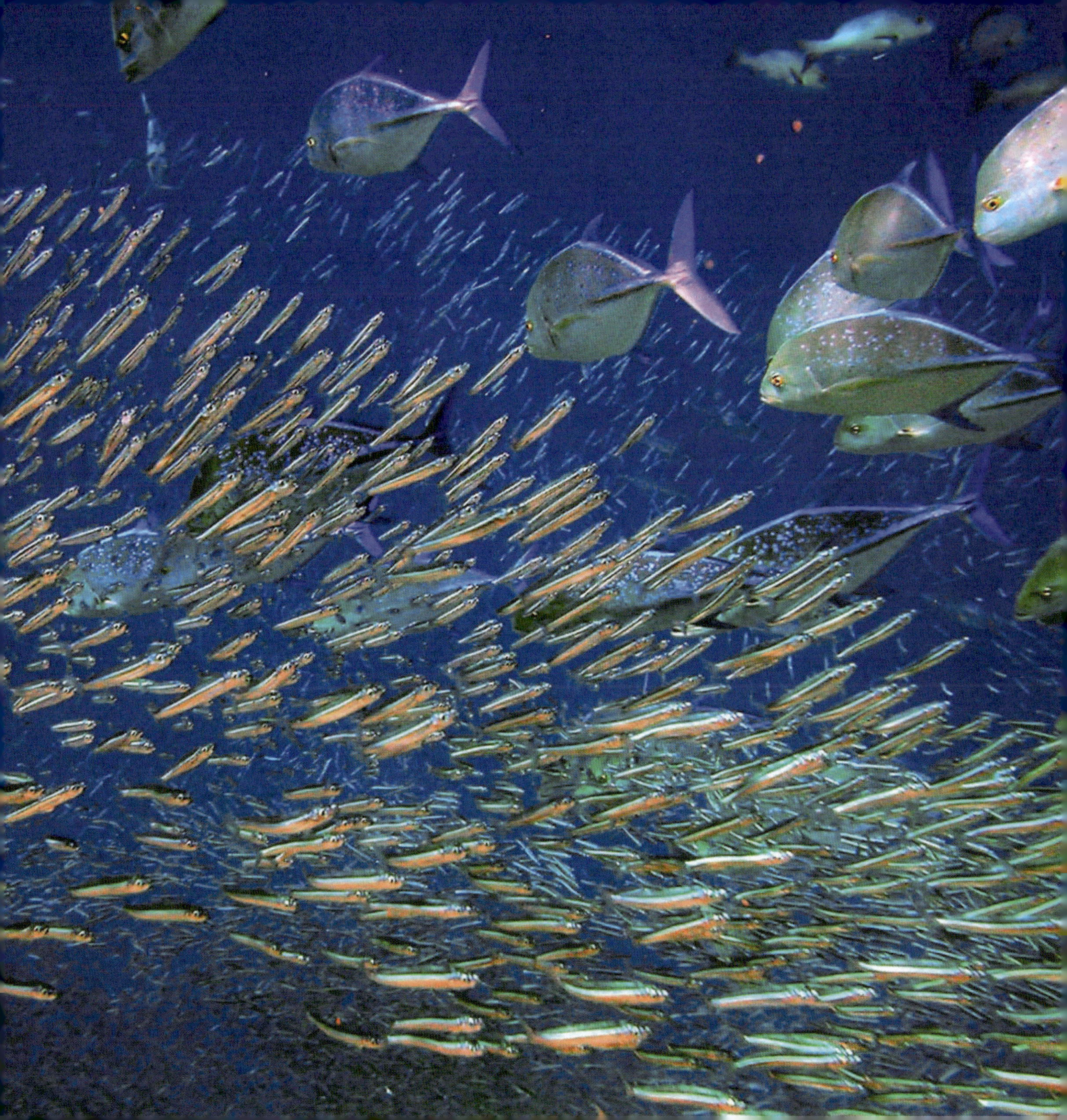

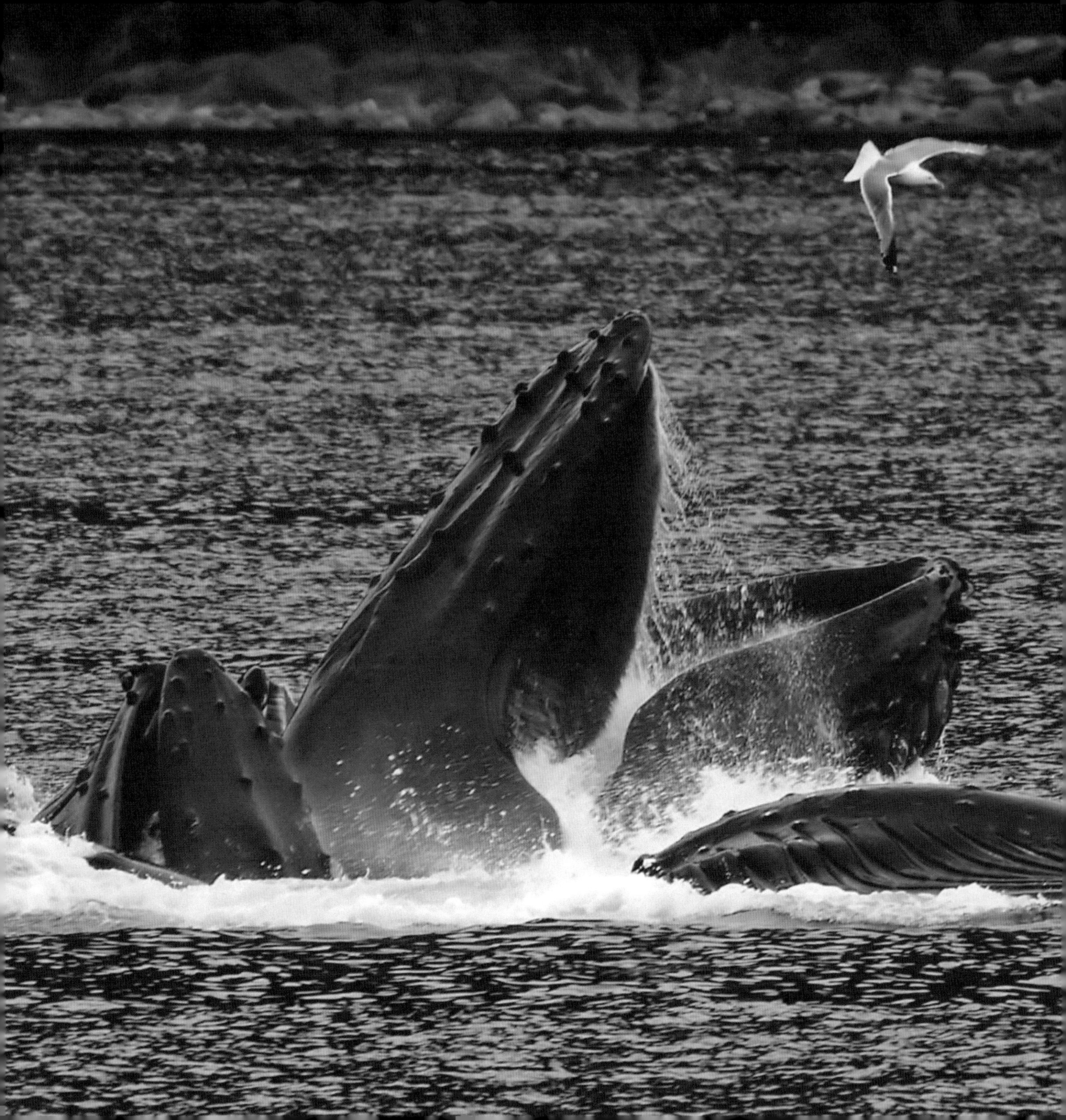

MARINE MAMMOLOGY

Most aspiring marine biologists are interested in mammals. This category contains the study of whales and dolphins. It also includes walruses, sea lions, and seals. So many people want to get into this field of marine biology that competition is stiff and it's difficult to get funding for research and experiments.

IDENTIFYING OCEAN SPECIES

Marine biologists have only begun the process of identifying all the species that exist in the environment formed by our interconnected ocean basins.

Although we think of them as separate, water from all the ocean basins flows back and forth, so you can think of the separate oceans as one big global ocean.

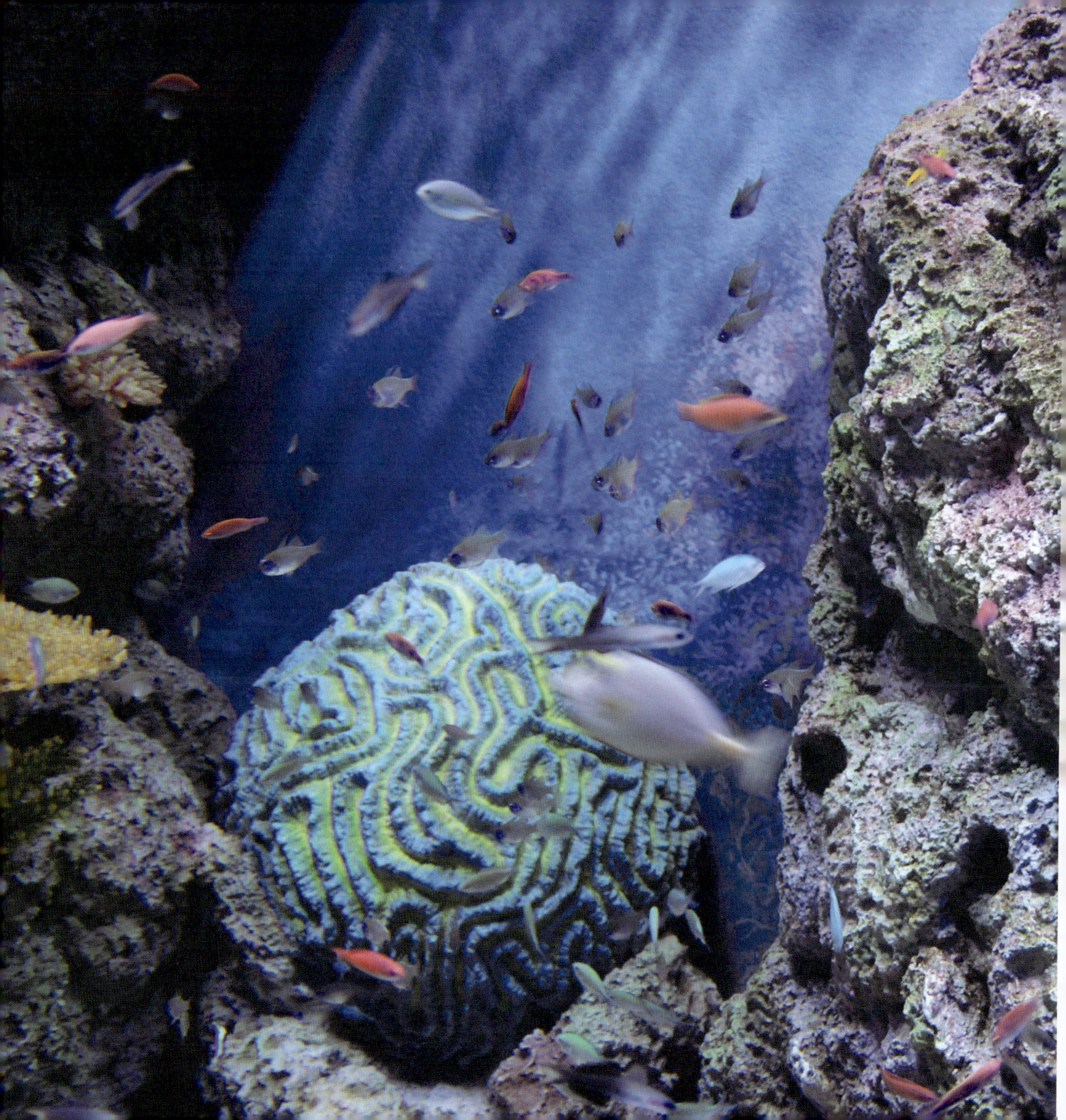

OCEAN HABITATS

The oceans are so vast that they encompass many different types of habitats. Marine creatures have adapted to every possible condition from hostile, cold temperatures to pressures that human bodies can't withstand. The pressure at the deepest ocean depth is equivalent to one person trying to hold more than 50 jumbo jets on top of each other. Because the global ocean is so vast it's hard to believe that humans could change it in any way, but we have.

Coral Planting

Every year, three times the amount of garbage as the weight of fish caught is thrown into the ocean. Both overfishing and pollution from human activity is having a seriously negative effect on the ocean's food chains.

Around the world, marine biologists and conservationists are working together to ensure ocean water stays healthy. The lives of marine organisms and our lives depend on keeping ocean water safe.

OCEAN CREATURES

There are over 200,000 identified species of marine organisms, but there are millions more that haven't been identified or cataloged yet. These animals and plants vary in size from microscopic to 98 feet (30 m) in length. Here are the major categories of ocean creatures that marine biologists study.

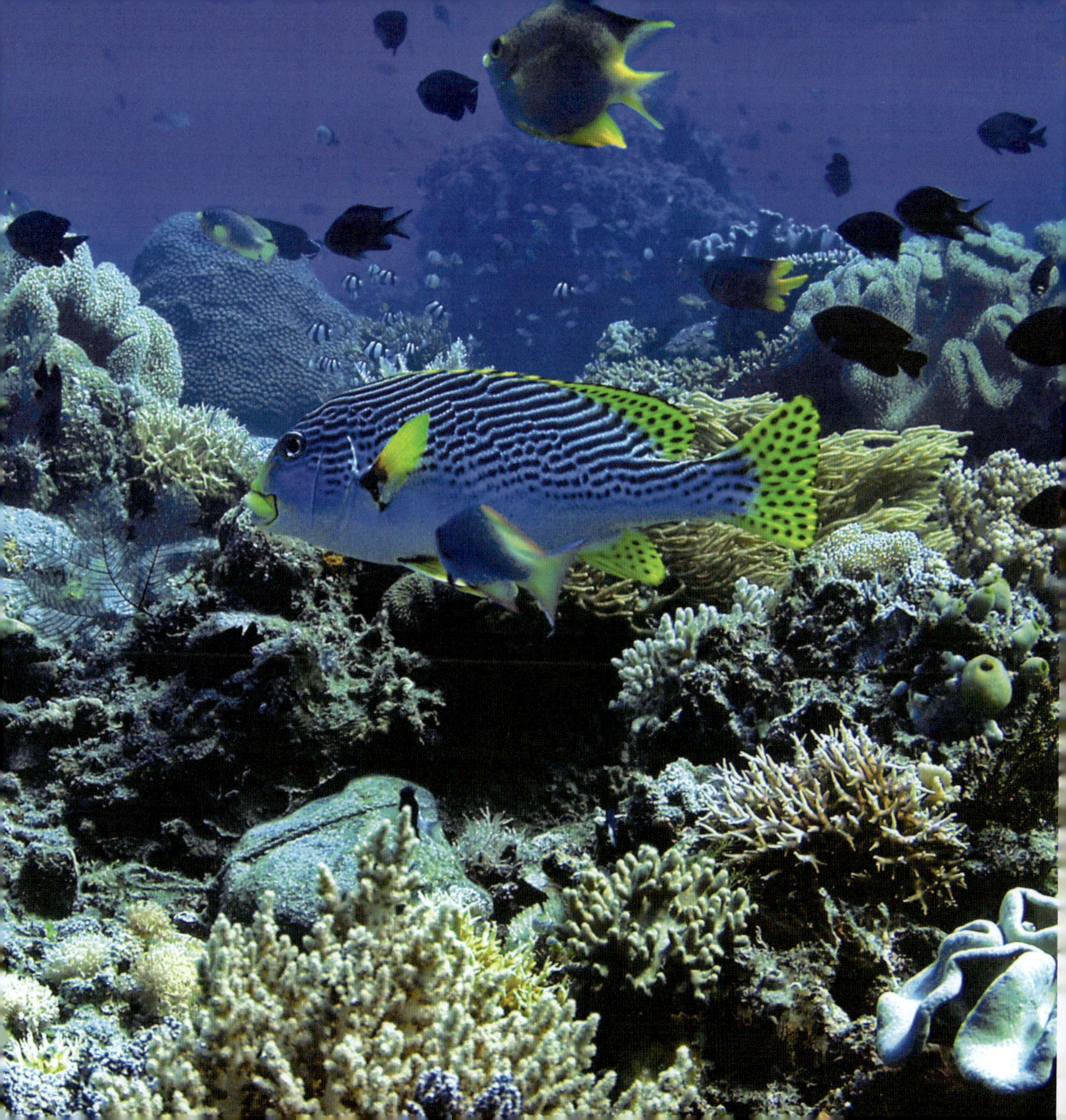

Cuttlefish

CEPHALOPODS AND CRUSTACEANS

⇨ **Octopuses,** squid, and cuttlefish fall into the category of cephalopods, which are invertebrate mollusks.

They have big heads and sets of arms with tentacles. Crustaceans, such as lobsters, shrimp, and crayfish, all have a hard shell around their bodies called an exoskeleton.

SEABIRDS

Birds are vertebrates, which means they have skeletons. They are warm-blooded and have feathers and wings.

They hatch from eggs. Seabirds, as compared with other types of birds, breed later in life and produce less offspring than birds that don't live by the sea.

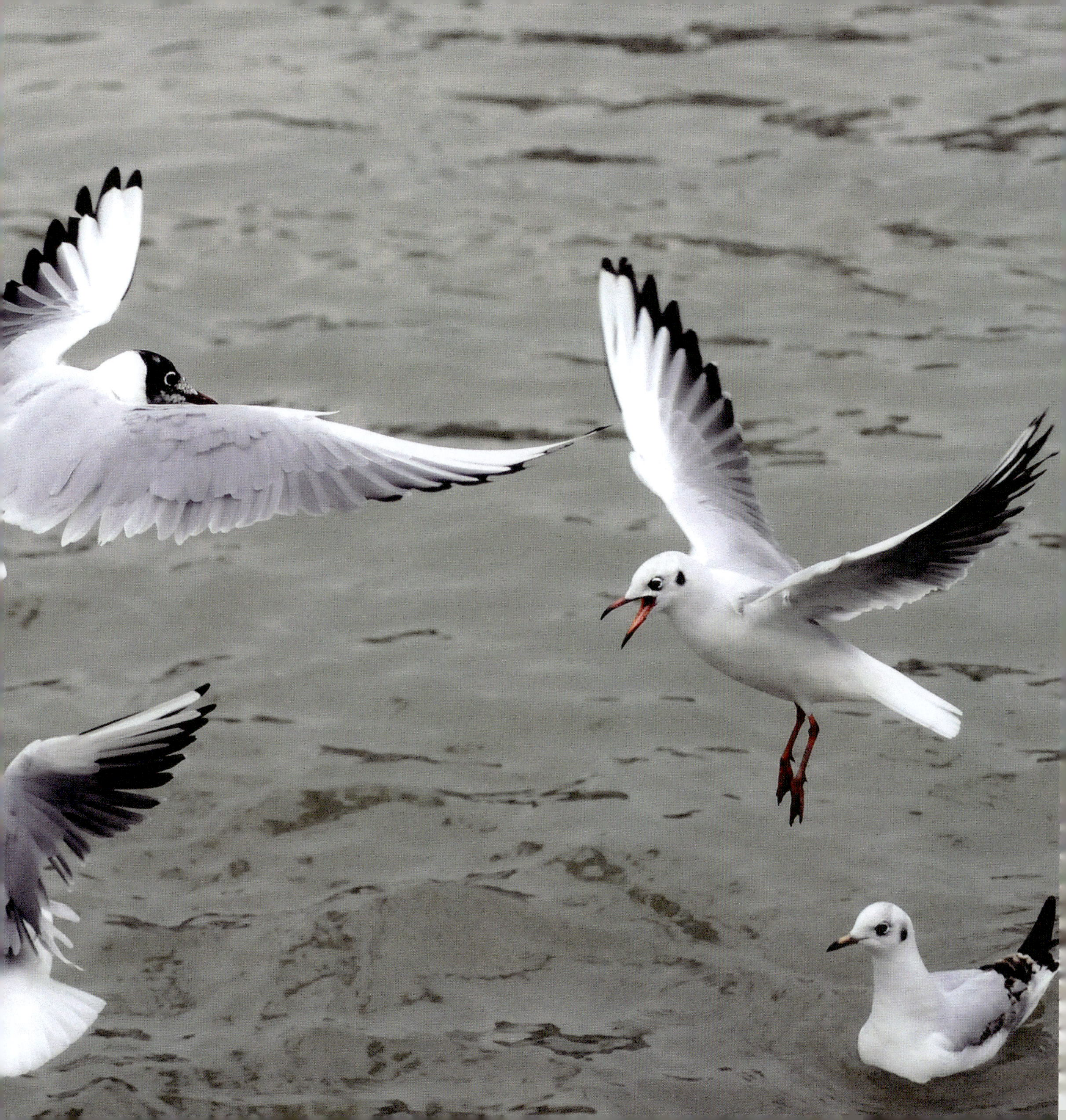

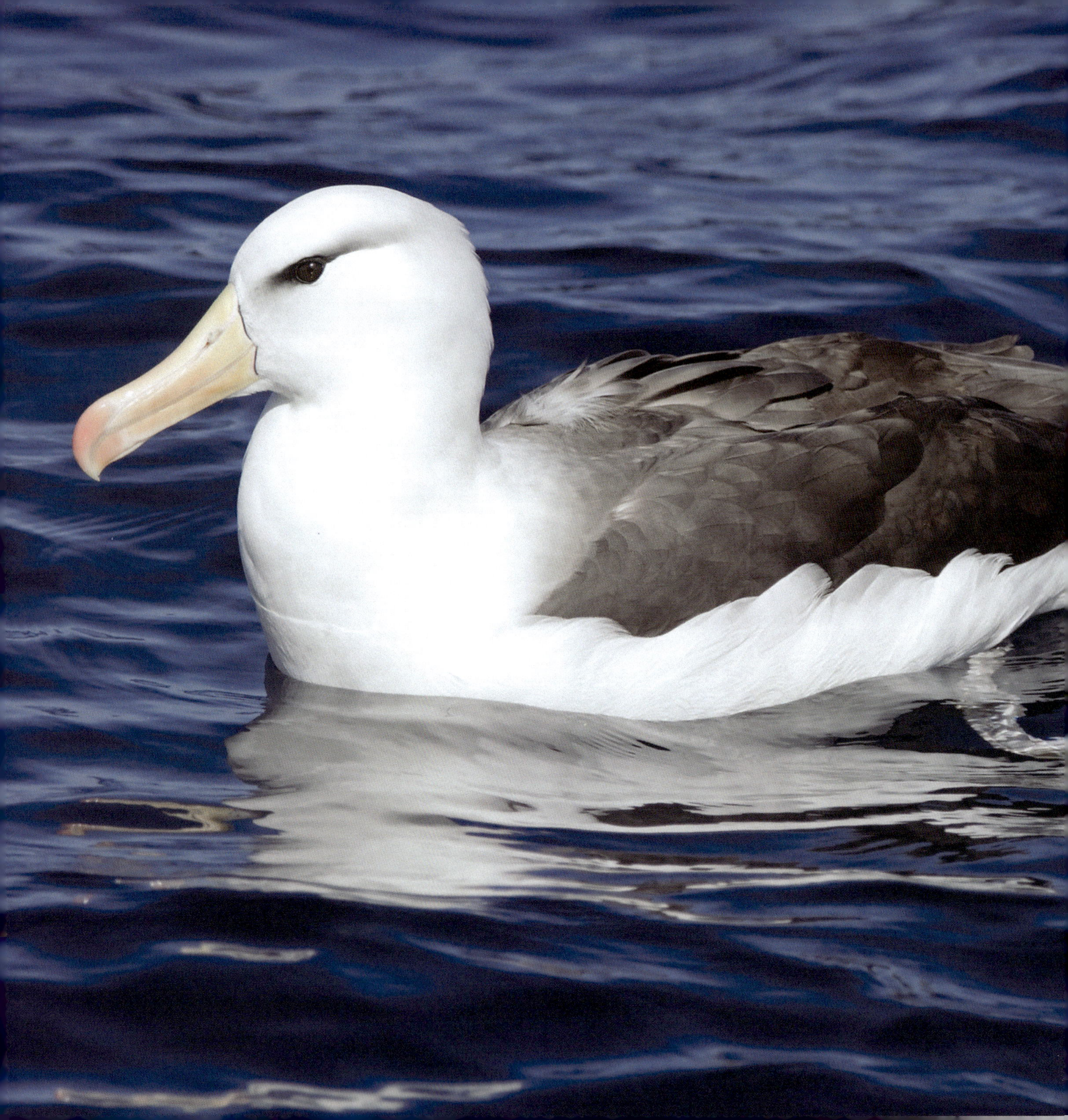

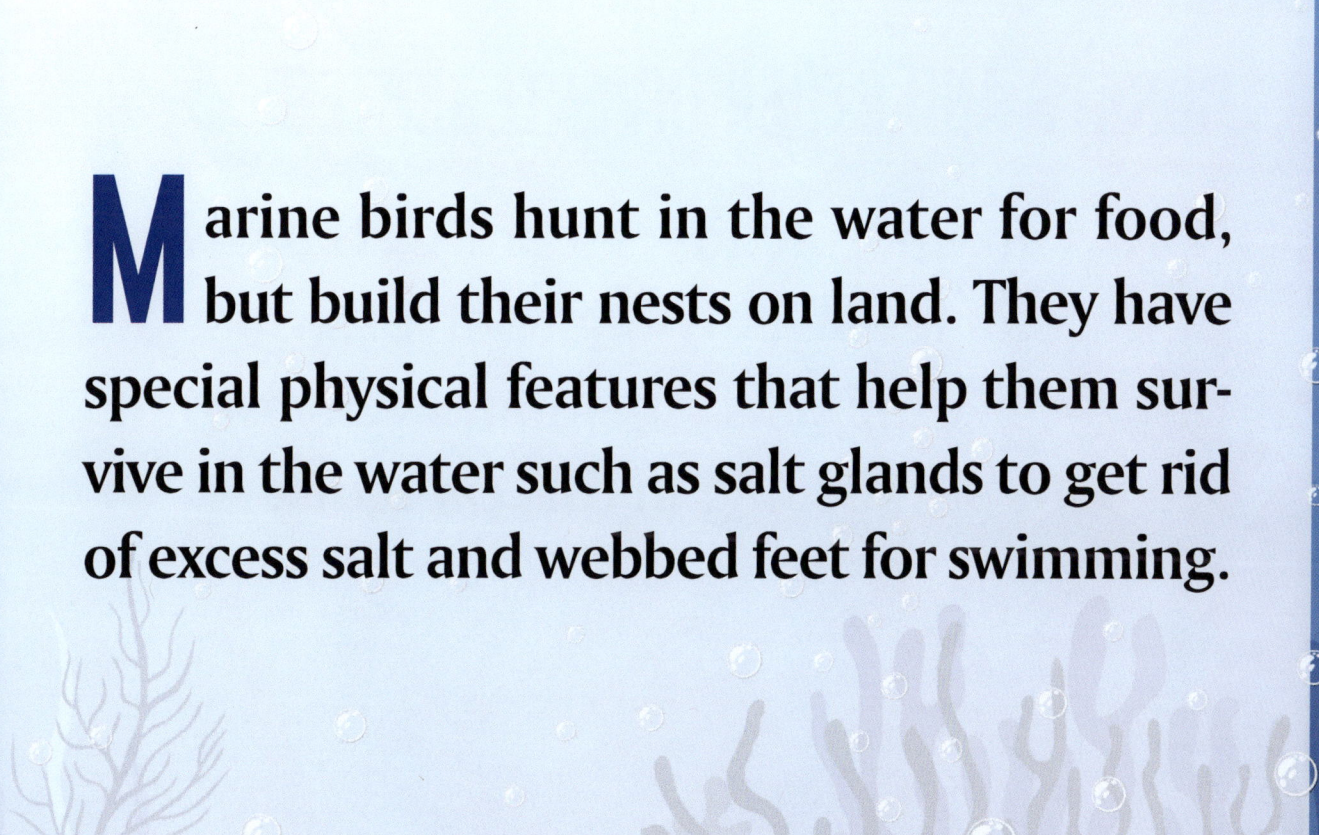

Marine birds hunt in the water for food, but build their nests on land. They have special physical features that help them survive in the water such as salt glands to get rid of excess salt and webbed feet for swimming.

CORALS AND OTHER INVERTEBRATES

Corals are marine invertebrates that live in tight colonies of individual polyps, which are tiny sac-like animals. Anemones, jellyfish, and sea pens also belong in this category.

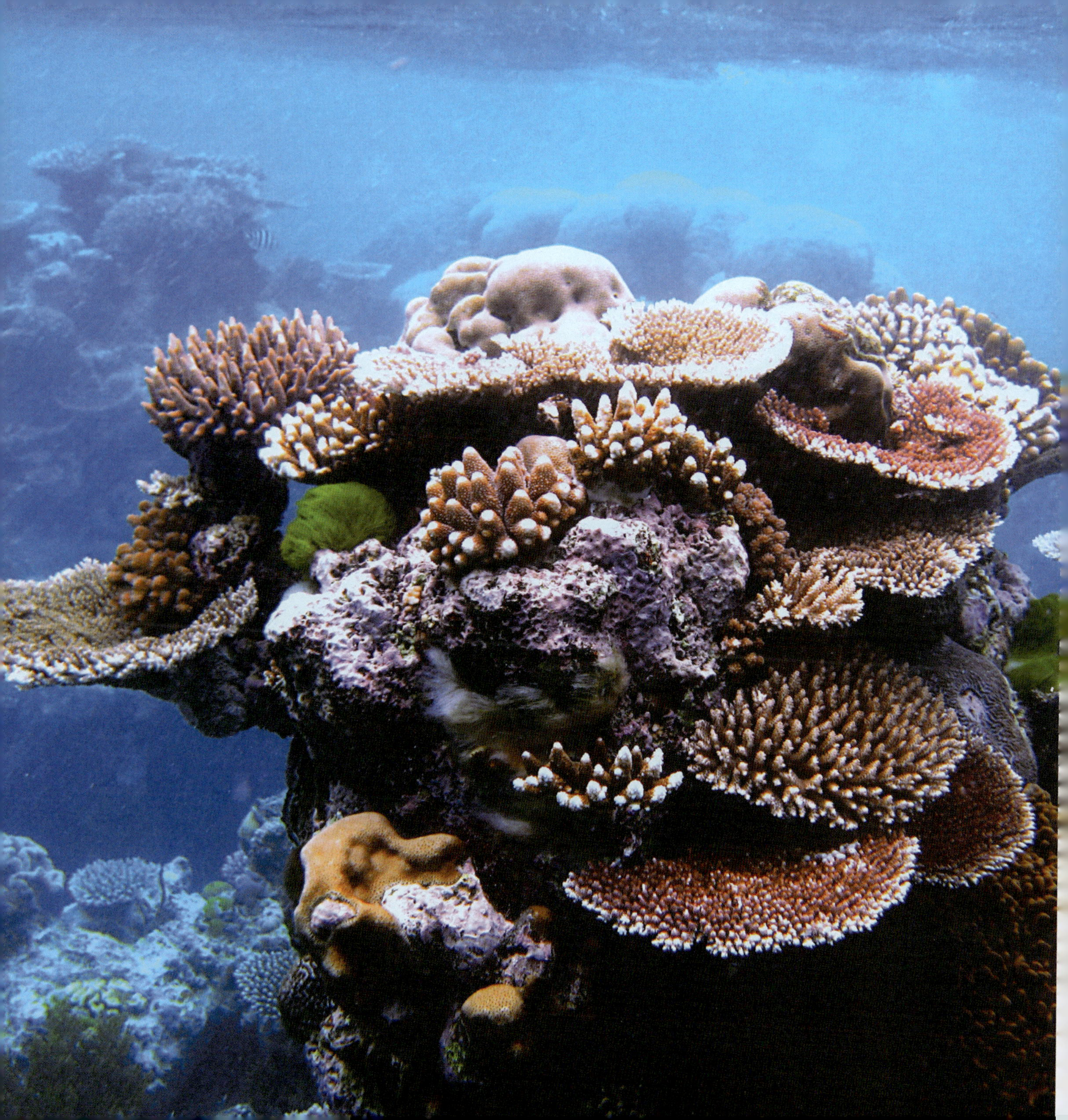

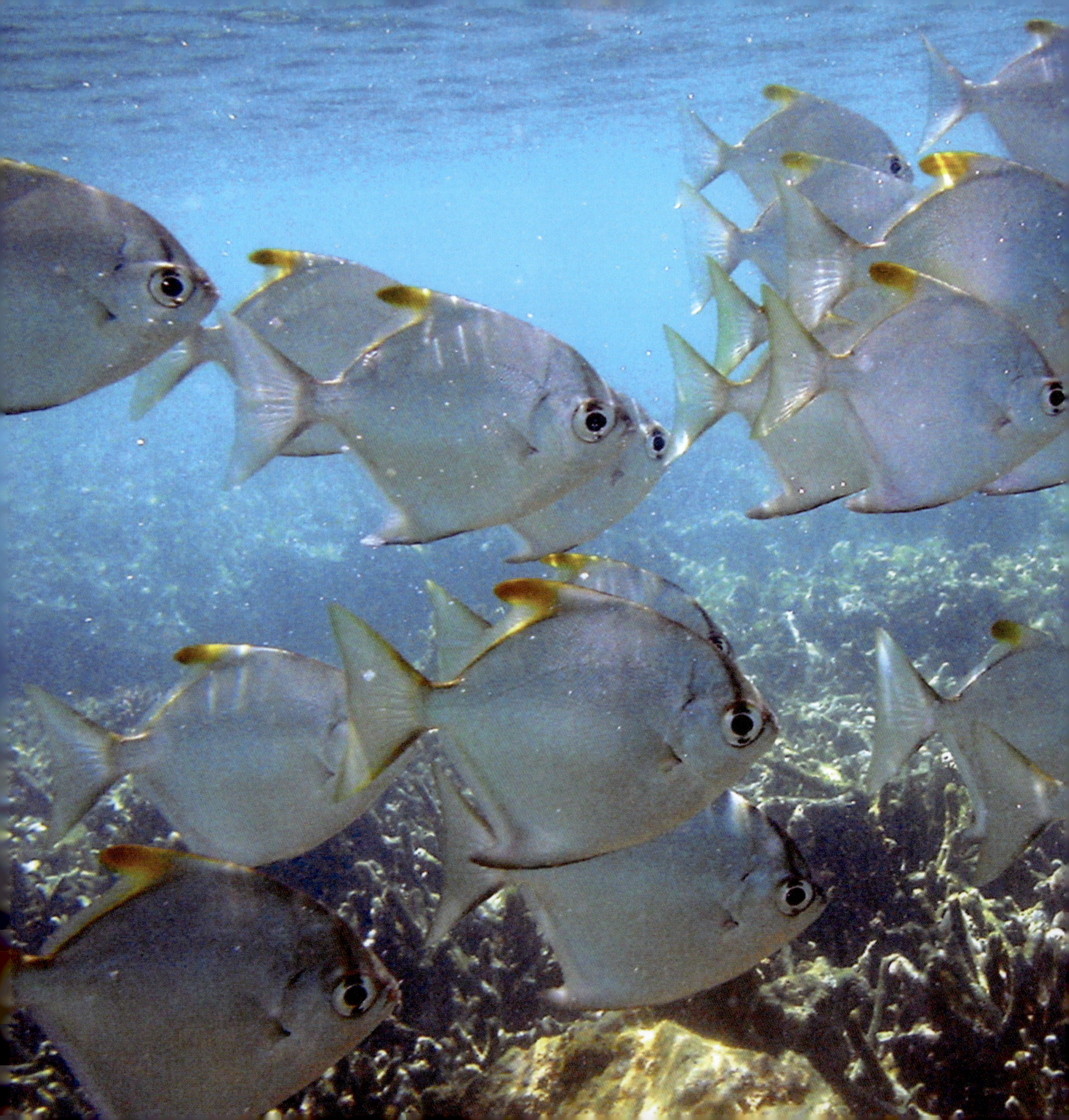

FISH

Fish are cold-blooded vertebrates. They can be found at every level of depth in the ocean. They don't have to come up to the surface for air because they take in air through their gills.

SHARKS AND RAYS

Sharks and rays are fish too, but they don't have bones like other fish. Instead, they have cartilage, which is more flexible than bone.

TURTLES AND REPTILES

Reptiles are cold-blooded vertebrates with lungs. They all have four legs except for sea snakes. They lay eggs and have scales on their bodies.

MAMMALS

Mammals are warm-blooded vertebrates. They give birth to live young and feed them milk. They breathe through lungs and must come up to the surface for air. Some marine mammals live on land part of the time.

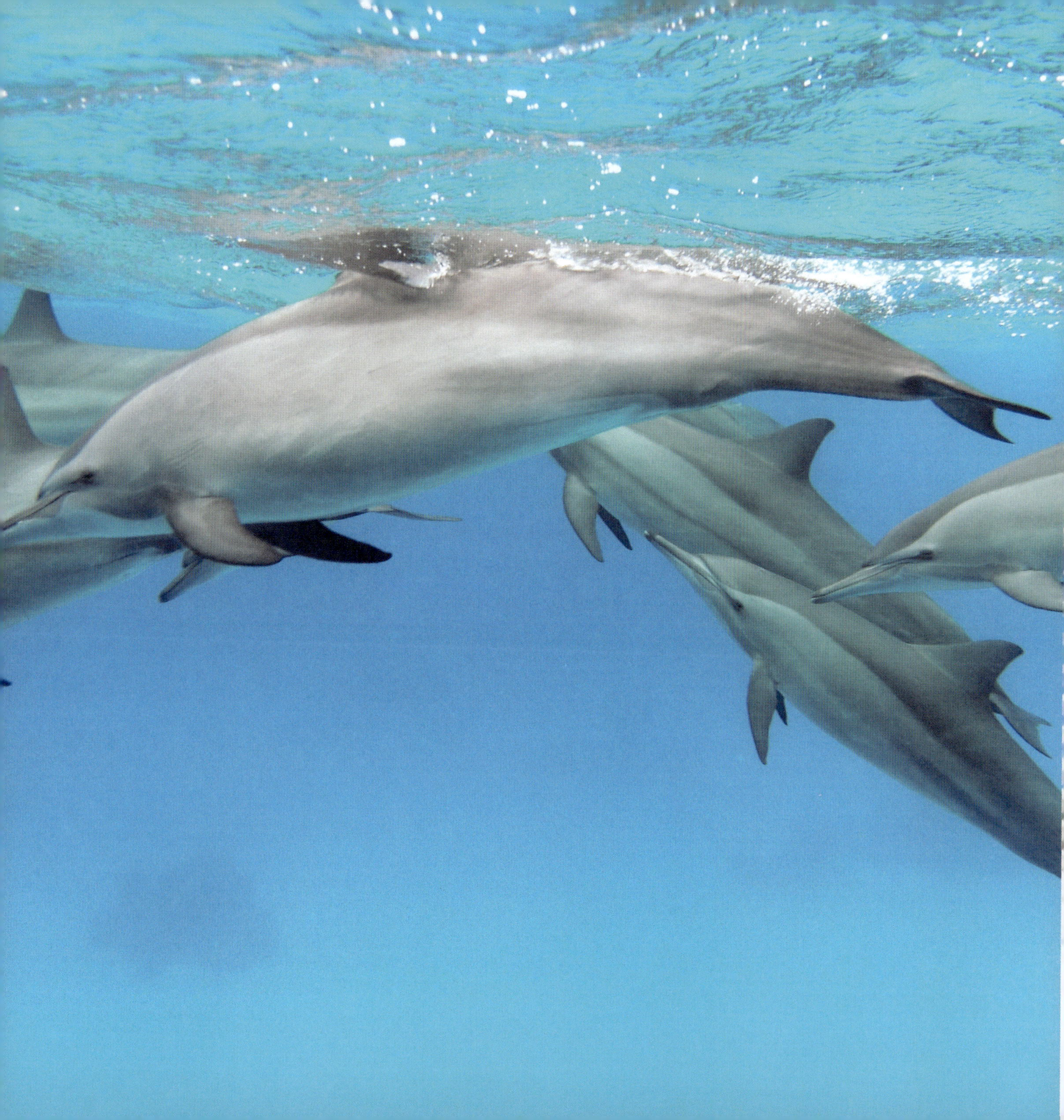

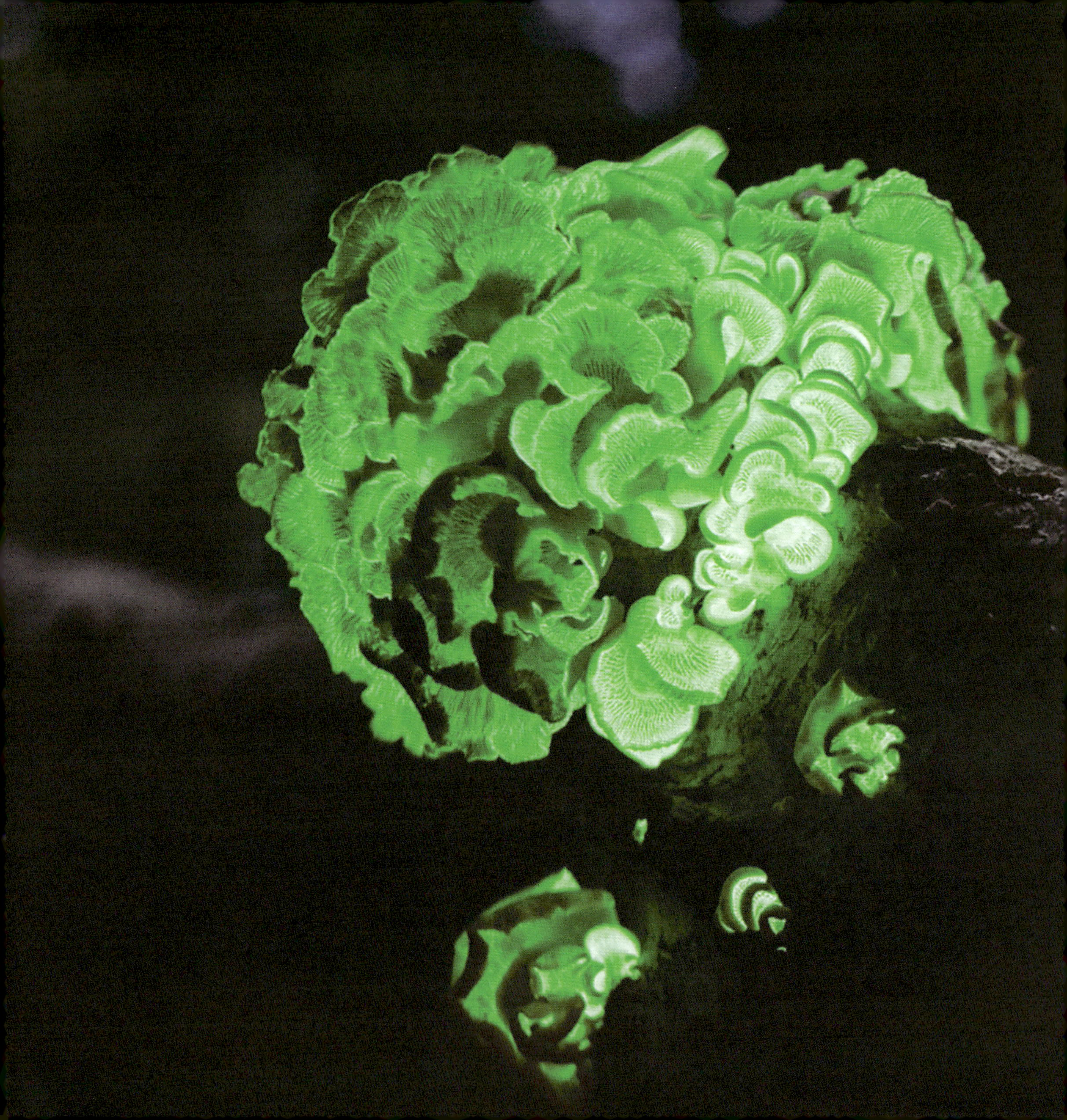

MICROBES

Bacteria, viruses, protozoa, and algae all belong in this category. Even though these creatures make up the largest biomass of all the categories, each individual creature can only be seen with a microscope.

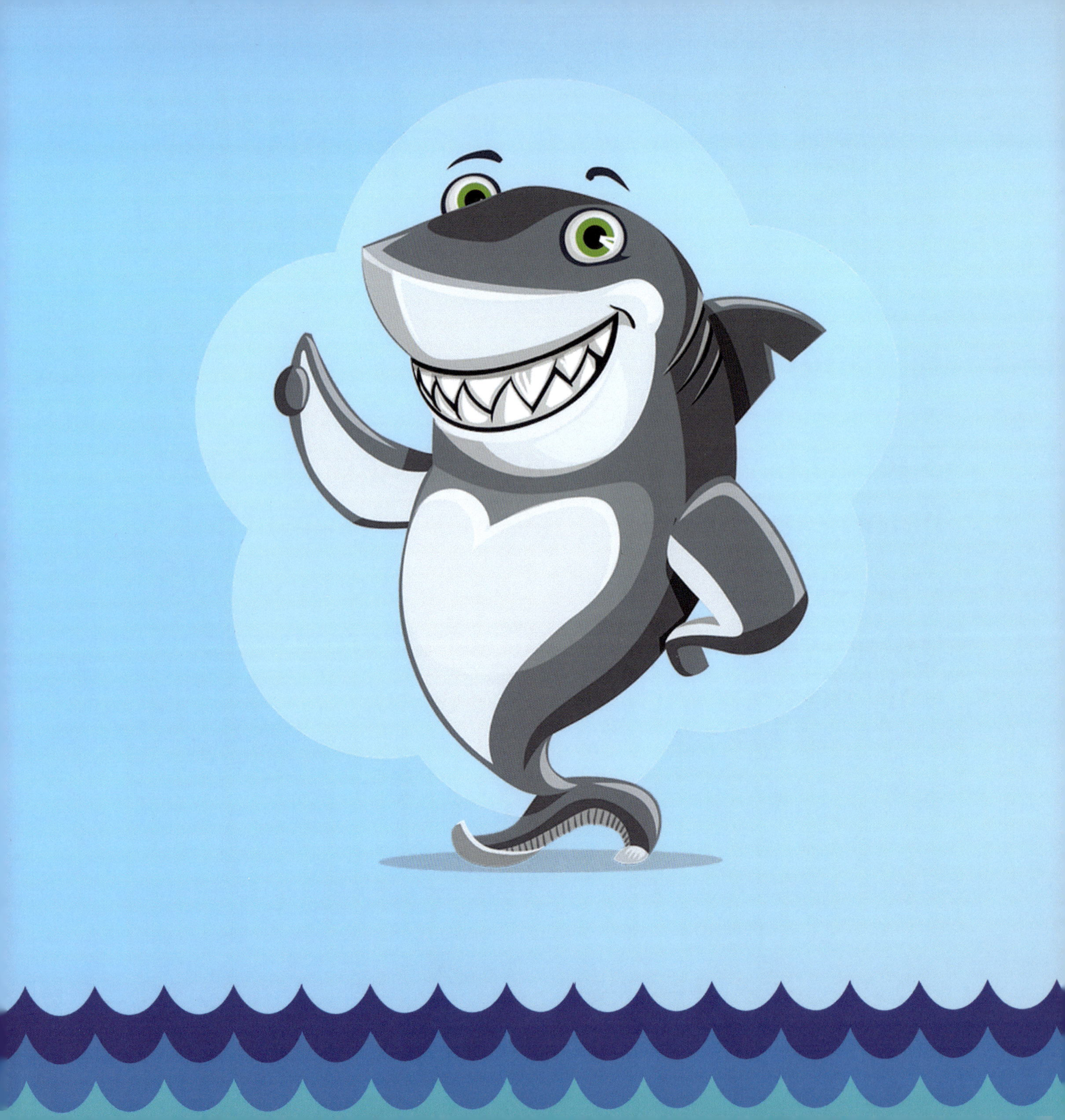

Awesome! Now you know more about all the types of animals and fish that marine biologists find in the water to study. You can find more Biology books from Baby Professor by searching the website of your favorite book retailer.

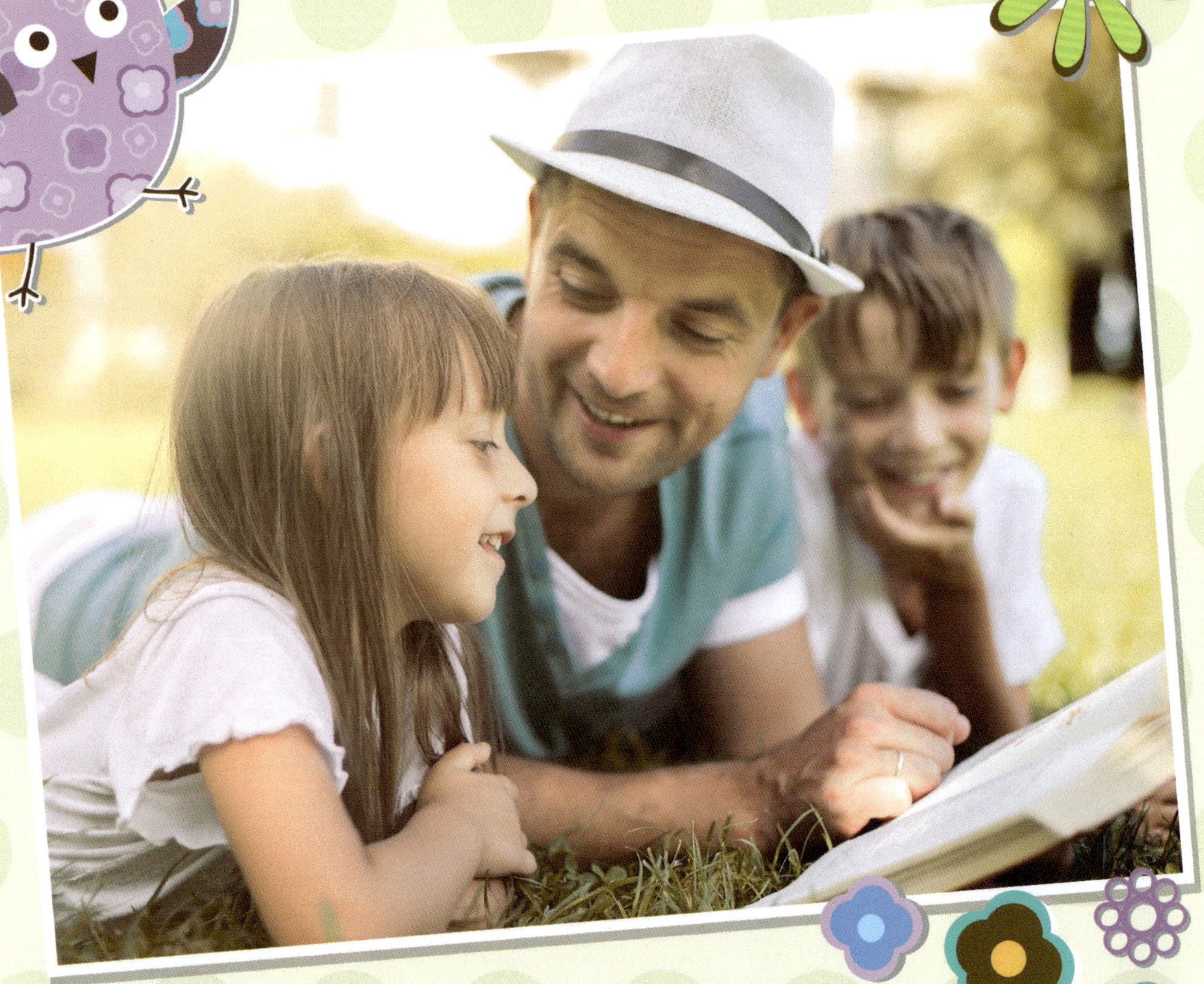

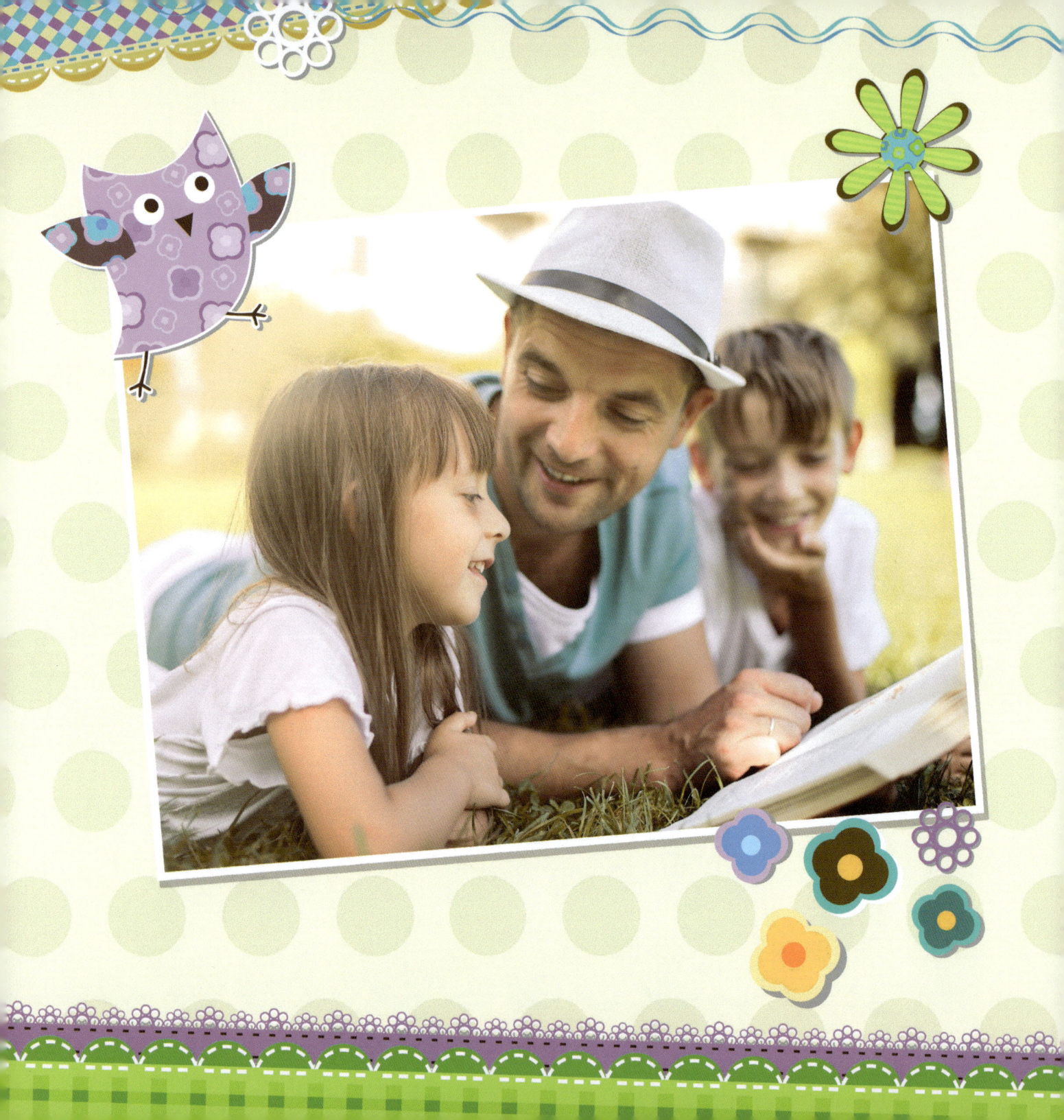

Visit

BABY PROFESSOR
EDUCATION KIDS

www.BabyProfessorBooks.com

to download Free Baby Professor eBooks and view our catalog of new and exciting Children's Books